THE PAULK

PERSPECTIVE

Delores Paulk

My name is Delores Paulk. I was born in 1950 to Jacob and Kathryn Buckwalter, who were missionaries in the state of Kentucky at the time.

I graduated from high school in 1968, did not attend college, and went right into the work force. In 1971 I met a man named Rev. Bill Drury, founder of a Christian Youth Organization called Teen Haven. In November of that same year I moved from the peaceful, rolling hills of Lancaster, Pennsylvania into the heart of North Philadelphia to work with him.

I spent seven years as a Bible teacher, camp counselor, rec room supervisor and bus driver. My experiences during that time opened my eyes and heart to a world I never knew existed.

When I left Teen Haven and moved as a single woman into the Germantown section of Philly, I met a Black man named Peter. Through many, many long conversations I learned about the history of Blacks in America and before slavery.

Thirty-six years and two kids later, we are still talking and I have a deep desire to share what I have learned with the hopes of introducing my readers to a whole new world of hope and understanding.

SOMETHING WORTH FIGHTING FOR

I drove up to the red light and stopped behind a small car. As I sat waiting for the light to change, a woman in the back seat of the car opened the door and threw out a small bag. It rolled over to the curb and stopped, adding yet another color to the litter already rainbowing the neighborhood.

My first impulse was to jump out and tell her she shouldn't mess up the street like that with her trash. My second thought was to keep quiet. A person who disregards Mother Earth's right to be litter free wasn't likely to appreciate a reprimand from a stranger.

So I went with my second thought and said nothing.

Then I started thinking about a movie I saw called "Zooman." A gangster had just killed a little girl and nearly everyone in the neighborhood knew he had done it. Yet no one spoke up for fear of retaliation. Zooman shared his private thoughts with the viewer several times and each one of his segments ended with him saying, "Ain't noboby said nothing." In his mind, since no one ever said anything to stop him, nobody really cared. So he kept committing one crime after another because nobody said nothing.

Then I thought about why I hadn't said anything to the woman in the car in front of me. The reasons were clear. I was unsure of the reaction I would get and unwilling to face uncertain consequences. I wasn't likely that I'd get "Thank you for pointing that out. I'll try to be more careful." I was more likely to get a "Mind your business white bitch," maybe a push or even a physical threat.

So, as most of us have learned to do, I "bit my tongue" to save my skin. I'm not sure whether this is good, bad or neutral. After all, I have a family to care for. I can't take unnecessary risks, can I?

But yet, I tell myself there must be some things in life worth speaking up about. Some things worth taking risks for. Some things worth living – even dying for.

Rosa Parks must have thought so. Dr. King and Malcolm X must have thought so.

I've heard and read what hate mongers and racists are spewing out of their mouths. Where, I wonder, are the voices of reason? Where are the voices of those who have learned to get along? Have learned to love, have learned to overcome.

True, we must choose our battles carefully. But this is one battle that has chosen us. This time we cannot bite our tongues. This time we cannot save our skin. For that's the issue they have chosen.

THE RIGHT TOOLS

On a talk show about race relations someone in the audience stood up and said to the panel, "Stop preaching at us and tell us what we can do to make it better." Unfortunately, the esteemed panel of experts had few actual suggestions. I have put together a list of things that I believe every concerned white person can do to "make it better."

1. Guard your thoughts. Erase all negative. Propel all positive.
2. Read the true, unfiltered history of blacks, including before they were brought to America.
3. Hang pictures of black people in your home.
4. Fill your library with books and magazines by and about black people.
5. View videos by and about black people.
6. Attend multi-cultural community events whenever possible.
7. Invite black people into your home. Sit down. Talk. Ask questions of each other. Get to know each other as you really are, not as you are portrayed to be.
8. Tell yourself and your children that differences are O.K. They are necessary. Being different does not mean being better or worse. It just means being different.
9. Listen to and watch objectively all media portrayals of black people. Be careful and don't let them bias your opinion.
10. Go to church, synagogue, mosque, wherever and pray for racial understanding.
11. Walk away from ethnic jokes. Openly rebuke those who try to perpetrate misunderstanding and hatred.
12. Repeat daily, "I am no better than anyone else. We are all created equal."

MAKE THIS PERSONAL STATEMENT OF DETERMINATION

Today I determine that I will NOT be the one:

-to bury another human being's potential or shatter his dreams.

-to make another human being feel uncomfortable in my presence.

-to belittle, patronize, or dehumanize another human being.

-to blame someone else or ignore the problems of racism.

-to pass on racial stereotypes to my children.

Today I determine that I WILL be the one:

-to accept, love and embrace black people, not simply tolerate them.

-to respect, appreciate and encourage black people as my equals.

-to dispel the myths, and open the doors of communication between black and whites.

-to speak out against racism whenever and wherever I find it.

-to help bring this madness to its final end.

THE SPARKLE OF HUMANITY

I was delighted to read about Cardinal Bevilacqua's letter to his flock calling them to eradicate racism. It was especially timely for me because I had just read a chapter in a book that also spoke of racism in terms of it being a spiritual, not a physical matter.

The book was The Priesthood of All Believers written by James Luther Adams and it was published in 1986. James Adams refers to the "principality of pigment," saying that the more this principality favors the people of one pigment, the more it engenders resentment and resistance at the hands of the people of other pigments. And I believe we all know which pigment has been historically treated as the favored one.

In his Study of History, Volume 1, Arnold Toynbee offers strong support for his judgment. He has shown how race feeling has become a principality and power and a dominion, as a consequence of Western civilization over the face of the earth since the fifteenth century.

He points out that in all the countries of this expansion where White people from Western Europe have settled "cheek by jowl" with representatives of other races, there are three elements in the situation which between them go far toward accounting for the strength and virulence of Western race feeling in our time.

First, the white people have established an ascendancy over the people of other races with whom they have come to share their new homes.

Secondly, these white masters have almost everywhere abused their power in some way and in some degree.

Thirdly, they are haunted by a perpetual fear that someday the positions may be reversed; that by weight of superior numbers or by more successful adaptation to the local climate or by ability to survive in a lower level of subsistence or by readiness to do harder physical or intellectual work, the Man of Color may eventually bring the white man's ascendancy to an end and perhaps even establish an ascendancy of his own over the white man.

Adams states that the cost in human suffering that has been paid in the past to this principality of racism is incalculable and in the strict sense irredeemable. Resentment, self-hatred, aggression, the hardening of the heart, the sense of deprivation- so goes the catalog of suffering.

He encourages us to be open to the change that comes from the source of our origin and fulfillment.

Returning to the source of our origin sounds like the answer to me. For should we decide to return, we would indeed find our fulfillment. And once we are fulfilled, we no longer look down our noses at each other. And when we stop looking down our noses, we look people straight in the eyes. And when we look people straight in the eyes- guess what. We see the sparkle of humanity that the source of our origin put there – and it looks exactly like ours.

WHAT WHITES DON'T GET
ABOUT THE O.J. SIMPSON VERDICT

During the hours that followed the O.J. Simpson not guilty verdict, I began to understand what a unique perspective I have on the black-white separation in this country.

I was standing in the corner of an 8th grade classroom at C.W.Henry School in Mt. Airy, Pennsylvania watching the T.V. as the verdict was read. Immediately the students jumped up and down, shouted and cheered as though O.J. had just scored the touchdown of a lifetime.

Later, as I was watching Geraldo Rivera on television I discovered that he and many others were confused, angered and even disgusted with the elation felt by black Americans and did not understand how they could possibly cheer the not guilty verdict.

Where has everybody been? Don't white people get it? Black people have suffered injustice in this country, have been dehumanized, mistreated, raped and yes, murdered, for years and years and years. And who has ever paid a penalty?

Who paid for all the lynchings? Who paid for the stealing, buying and selling of human beings? Who paid for the destruction of an entire black civilization and the further destruction of the black male image? Who paid while the greatest fraud every perpetrated convinced millions of white people that blacks were inferior? Who paid for the beatings, the whippings, the maiming, the mental anguish, the loss of sanity? Who paid for the throw-downs, the set-ups, the shake-downs, the police shootings?

Let's be honest. Powerful white people have been getting away with murder in this country for years. Mafia kingpins pay huge amounts of money to defense lawyers while laughing in the face of the justice system. White drug dealers pay their attorneys millions to find legal loopholes, jump through them and go merrily on their way selling drugs that kill our children, while low-level street users of small amounts get sent to jail by the millions. Prominent, powerful white families have always been able to buy their freedom.

Deals made behind closed doors have always protected guilty parties from suffering the consequences for their crimes. For heaven's sake, even the Catholic Church paid hush money to prevent sex scandals from coming out into the open and tarnishing their reputation.

The best defense money can buy has never been available to the everyday common person, particularly if he or she is black. So now, one black man rises to the occasion, plays the game and beats the white man at his own game, playing by his own rules. Johnny Cochran did what he was hired to do. Other lawyers get patted on the back for doing it every day. Johnny gets criticized. Others are credited with their brilliance and their strategy. Johnny gets condemned. Par for the course. Many white men don't relish the thought of admitting a black man can be brilliant, powerful, strong and successful. They've spent too many years trying to keep him down.

President Clinton issued a statement that the thoughts and prayers of the nation should be with the families of the victims. But where are the thoughts and prayers of the nation when a black child dies on the city streets? Where are the thoughts and prayers of the nation when a young, promising black man gets shot down on his front steps? Where are they when a black woman gets raped and murdered in a back alley? Where are they when gangsters violently control entire neighborhoods, forcing good, decent black people to live in fear every day of their lives? Most white don't see. Most whites don't care. Most whites don't listen. Most whites don't pray. And most whites don't even make an effort to understand.

I don't think Blacks should be expected to cry over the deaths of two white people. They've experiences the untimely, violent death of loved ones over and over again for years and years and years, and the nation has looked the other way.

When a white serial killer is caught, the first thing we see on T.V. is a psychiatrist explaining the killer's childhood. His father beat him, his mother molested him, he was teased by other kids, etc. We are supposed to be convinced that a white person capable of violence is rare and that there is always some explanation for it. But let a black man commit a crime and immediately it is assumed that "black people are violent" or "that's just the way those people are."

Many white Americans think that Black problems are created by Blacks and that they are only suffering the consequences of their own behavior. Let's face reality here. Black people were brought to this country forcefully and violently by white people. If you don' believe the white race has been the most violent, greedy, power-hungry race in the world, ask a Native-American Indian, if you can find one.

The situation in which Blacks find themselves was created for them. Redlining, fear tactics, segregation, lies about their mental capabilities, oppression – this stuff was all done to Black people, inflicted upon them, not caused by them.

Black people in this country are not responsible for the nation's mess. White people created it and I believe white people should apologize for it and get on with the business of reconciliation. I liked what an older white lady said on T.V. right after the verdict. She said, "Maybe one man, who I believe may even be guilty, has to be set free to bring about a change in this society."

I stand in the schoolyard weekday mornings and listen to the students recite the Pledge of Allegiance to the flag. It always ends the same way, "With liberty and justice for all." And I've always wondered if it will ever really be true.

Today I am more hopeful than ever that the students at this school and every other school in the nation will soon be able to say those words and mean them. One Black man said it on T.V. after the verdict. "I feel like now we've got a chance." I say it's about time.

GET TO KNOW EACH OTHER

I received many responses to my letter about the O.J. Simpson verdict. Some of the responses made me realize that people had assumed that I was black. It didn't occur to me to mention that I am a blonde haired, blue eyed white woman. This fact, I believe is what makes my perspective unique.

In 1971 I moved from Lancaster County, Pennsylvania into the heart of a North Philadelphia ghetto to work with a Christian Youth Organization. One of my first memories of that move is a little black kid throwing a can at me while I thought, "What have I ever done to him?"

I had my purse and my favorite sneakers stolen, my room broken into more than once, and my personal safety threatened on numerous occasions.

In 1975 I was attacked from behind by a black man. He stuck a knife to my throat and said, "Get in the car white bitch or I'll cut your fuckin throat.

In 1978 I was thrown down a flight of stairs by a black teenager who threatened to rape and kill me.

Since my move to Germantown in 1979 I have been called white ass, white bitch and white trash. In 1989 an angry black woman threatened to kill me. In 1993 a hostile black teenage girl threatened to bash my head in with her shovel and bury my white ass in the snow.

Contrary to some recently expressed opinions of my character, however, these experiences have not served to make me a hateful person. Rather they have served to make me wonder what on earth has driven people to such extreme behaviors. They have served to make me strong, cautious and determined to do what I can to bridge the gap between black and white people in this city and in our nation.

I remember clearly one day in 1971 before I moved to Philadelphia. I was sitting in my parent's dining room. I was looking at a picture of a convicted black criminal on the front page of a newspaper. Uncontrollable tears rolled down my face. I had no idea what I was crying about at the time. I had no idea what God had in store for me.

Over the many years I've lived in Philadelphia I have come to understand many things. One of them is best described by Nathan McCall, author of Makes Me Wanna Holler. He says, "There is nothing wrong with black men. There is something wrong with the forces that have shaped their lives."

Nathan McCall also believes that if people are given the right information they will come to the right conclusions. I believe it is time for white people to gather the right information. It is time to erase from our minds all the negative images written there by our whitened version of history. It is time to rewrite it in truth, beginning with the glorious history of blacks before slavery and moving to the marvelous accomplishments of blacks since and in spite of slavery.

I have found this written dialogue most interesting and revealing. Some of the people who wrote responses to my essay attacked my person, my morals, my character and my opinion without even knowing who I am. Their reactions were clearly based on the negativity in their own minds and opinions they had already formed about black people in general and about O.J. Simpson in particular.

Making assumptions about people without really knowing them is what this thing is all about.

We must begin to know each other as we really are. We, as white people, must forget what we've always thought about black people. We must forget what we've seen on TV or read in newspapers about black people. We must put into perspective any unpleasant incidents we've had with black people. For we cannot and must not judge an entire race of people based on the negative actions of certain individuals within that race. Do we judge our own race so?

Finally, we must talk with black people – not about them, not to them, not at them – but with them. And we must learn to listen.

Charles Caleb Colton said, "We hate some people because we do not know them: and we will not know them because we hate them." I think it can also be said that we fear some people because we do not know them and we will not know them because we fear them.

We, as white people must have a fundamental change of heart. Our feelings towards black people must change from contempt or tolerance or hate to genuine acceptance and love. Only then will we see the walls that divide us some crashing down.

Hatred built that horrible dividing wall one brick at a time. And that's how love must destroy it. One brick at a time. I truly believe that the hammer is in our hands, white America. The hammer is in our hands.

ANGER

One written response to my O.J. letter said that I was very angry and hate-filled, but I don't believe we can equate anger with hatred. Of course I have some anger, but expressing that anger does not mean that I am full of hate or that I encourage anyone else to be.

Most married folks have been angry with their spouse at one time or another. Most parents have been angry with their children. But being angry at them does not mean that we hate them. Indeed, we continue to feel the opposite – we continue to love them- through the anger and beyond. Do we stop loving our spouses while we're angry at them? No, we love them through it all, right up to the make- up kiss. Do we stop loving our children when we chastise them? No, it is because of that love that we chastise them in the first place.

Lots of black people are angry, and with good reason. But how free are they to express that anger? How much have they held back and for how long? Several people said to me recently that they have wanted to say the things I said in my letter but were afraid to do so. When black people express their anger over slavery they've been told to forget about it. That was years ago. We're tired of hearing about the past. Stop blaming your troubles on somebody else. Pull yourselves up by your own bootstraps, etc., etc.

I think that eventually people stopped expressing themselves and held it in because they always got the same answer. They were told how to think, how to feel and how to respond to something that was done to their ancestors. And all the while they watch other groups hold annual prayer vigils in order to "remember the past, so that we do not repeat it."

While some folks think we should forget the past, others, like me, believe we should apologize for it. The Southern Baptist Convention passed a resolution apologizing for supporting racism for much of its history. It reads in part, "We unwaveringly denounce racism in all its forms, as deplorable sin; and that we lament and repudiate historic acts of evil such as slavery from which we continue to reap a bitter harvest."

Some readers responded to my letter by saying that I should not see color. To them, I say this. That's an easy thing to suggest. But I, as a White person, have never felt the pangs from the stares, the negative vibes from the body language, the rejection from the crossing to the other side that many black people have felt. Every time a white person inches away, screws up their face, follows customers around the store, pulls someone over because he looks suspicious, assumes a child can't learn, passes over someone for a promotion, pays someone less money for the same job, clutches a purse or quickly locks a car door, it is a reminder that for many white people, color still matters. And I don't think we can get past it until we face it.

I must finally say that I see a big difference between placing blame and telling the truth. People who refuse to hear and accept the truth have no hope of finding solutions to their differences. People who embrace the truth, no matter how painful or self-revealing it may be, will ultimately find themselves set free.

DIVIDED

In 1968, Lyndon B. Johnson received The Kerner Report from the National Advisory Commission on Civil Disorder as an explanation for the riots and rage of the 60s.

The report stated clearly that: "Certain fundamental matters are clear. Of these, the most fundamental is the racial attitude and behavior of White Americans toward Black Americans. Race prejudice has shaped our history decisively; it now threatens to affect our future. White racism is essentially responsible for the explosive mixture which has been accumulating in our cities since the end of WWII."

The report concluded that America is divided into two societies – one Black and one White – both separate and unequal, and the primary cause evolves from white racism.

The Kerner Report said that whites, not blacks were responsible for the restlessness. White people were responsible through their treatment of and attitude towards black people.

I know, many white people say they've never done anything to black people. They blame black people for their own problems. But I personally don't see how an oppressed people can be blamed for their reaction to years of mistreatment and dehumanization. White people have told black people for years that they are only 3/5 human, assuming they are 2/5 animal or savage. Why then does violent behavior surprise them? Whey then does self-destructive behavior surprise them? Why then are they surprised when life has little or no meaning to people who have been told for years that their life is not worth living?

The only thing that surprises me is how we as white people can remain so blind and unrepentant. We, collectively, are responsible for the cruelest, most savage crimes in history and we have never confessed, apologized or made amends. I believe it's time for that to change.

RODNEY KING

I watched and listened to a lot of news shows reporting on the aftermath of the not guilty verdict in the beating of Rodney King. One reporter said he thought the President, Congress and Fortune 500 could make a difference by beginning to create a more economically balanced society. I wholeheartedly agreed but decided not to hold my breath while waiting for them to make a move.

Then the reporter was asked by the anchorman what individuals can do to improve race relations in this country. His answer was "I don't know."

On this point, I do have a suggestion. Our nation's problems stem from negativity. I believe individuals must change this into positivity.

When I was a child I was taught in church that I have two natures within me constantly at war with one another. One good, one bad. To help me visualize this I was told to picture two dogs inside of myself. One black. One white. The black dog was my bad nature. The white dog was my good nature. Whichever dog I fed the most, I was told, would win out over the other because he would be stronger. I suppose the concept was alright, but why did they color the dogs black and white? Why did they color them at all?

Of course, as I grew up, there were other negative things. Good guys wear white hats. Bad guys wear black hats. Black as night – boogie man, black cat, witches wearing black hats, and so on. I heard black people called niggers. Heard jokes about them. Was told they were lazy, dirty, violent, over sexed. You name it, I heard it. I was even told by church people to stay away from black people. "They need the gospel too, dear, but we just can't associate with them," I was told.

I do not and cannot to this day remember hearing anything positive about black people during my childhood. Not anything.

And now that I'm giving it thought, it was because people that I knew didn't know any black people. They were like parrots – repeating what they'd heard. The negative stereotypes. Repeating and reteaching the negative images born of fear and ignorance. And never feeling bad about it. Never realizing the damage being done. Never realizing the negative vibrations being sent out from their brains, and being picked up by some wide open, absorbing, innocent child.

If negativity can cause so much damage, imaging what positivity could do. Imagine positive thoughts – positive vibrations, filling the air.

We have got to change our thought patterns. Negative thoughts produce negative feelings which produce negative behavior. Positive thoughts produce positive feelings which lead to positive behavior.

We cannot allow negative thoughts to stay in our minds. Maybe we can't always prevent them from coming in. Maybe they pop in uninvited. But when they come we've got to get them out – immediately. Shout them out. Talk them out. Pray them out. Sing them out. But get them out.

Negativity will destroy us all. Positivity will save us. Shall we live or shall we die? I believe it's up to individuals. Individuals like you and me.

During the L.A. riots a light-skinned black guy was attacked by a black mob. He later suggested: "There's a certain point at which people cease to be victims of society and become the victims of their own stupidity. If you can't ask yourself if what you're doing is right or wrong …if you just go along with the crowd, you keep yourself in a small and limited world."

RACISM: THE ELEPHANT IN THE ROOM

A friend of mine asked me what I thought of the two 18 year old
white kids accused of killing their infant. Their attorney said that
because they had not actually been convicted of any crime, they got
to go home. I just shook my head. Then she said, "Tell me this. Do
you think if they'd been black that they'd be home? I rolled my eyes
and said, "What do you think?"
She said, "Isn't it something? Everybody knows this. But it's like
there's an elephant in your living room and nobody wants to talk
about it. Everybody just walks around it like it's not even there."
Her description reminded me of the way I'd often felt while living in
the peaceful Bible Belt of Lancaster County, Pennsylvania. It was
like there was this "thing" hanging in the air – everybody knew it –
but no one wanted to admit it or discuss it openly.
As great and as powerful a nation as we are – we are pathetic when it
comes to dealing with the realities of how this country treats black
people.
The elephant in our collective living room sprays out waters of
hatred, tramples on justice and suffocates equality. And still we feed
the elephant! We fatten him with daily doses of silence, apathy,
noncommittal and denial. We strengthen him with long held
prejudices, stereotypical attitudes, and stubborn resistance to change.
We coddle the elephant as though his presence protects us from
ourselves. From the racism engrained in our consciousness since the
day we were born. From the seeds of superiority planted in us
before we even began to grow. From the false sense of security that
says everything is going to be all right. From the lie that says to
ignore the problem and it will eventually go away.
And so, one dark night while we sleep we will be awakened by the
thunderous crash of falling walls, shattering glass and tumbling
beams. For the elephant of racism will have finally grown too big.

WHAT WE DON'T KNOW CAN HURT US

I read an opinion column that stated, "Since many traditional history books written by the white majority society in the past have excluded or distorted information about certain aspects of slavery, readers are often misinformed and thus miseducated."

In my case, that's putting it mildly. I can, to this day, remember one particular page of my high school history book. In the lower left hand corner there was a picture of slaves picking cotton. The paragraph above it said that black people were brought to the U.S. from Africa and that they picked cotton every day. The following paragraph said that while they picked cotton they sang songs, and that's how we got Negro spirituals.

And that was the extent of my education on American slavery days. As I got older and realized that there were problems relating back to slavery days, I remember thinking, "It didn't look so bad."

But little did I know of the real suffering that was inflicted on black people when they were taken from their homeland and brought to these shores. I knew nothing of the ships where men were literally thrown in on top of each other, many getting desperately sick and others dying on the long voyage to the slave owners plantations. I knew nothing of the islands where they were taken to be "made into slave," where things like cutting open pregnant women were used to instill fear in their hearts and force them to submit. I knew nothing of the tricks used to pit one black man against another while bowing down to the white man. I knew nothing of the separation of families, the breeding of strong, muscular men for field work and the distinct differences created between "field niggers" and "house niggers."

But now with the helpful guidance of a loving husband and reading books I never even knew existed, I am beginning to see. My eyes are beginning to open and see the truths that have been hidden from me for most of my life. And now that they are open, I will never close them to these truths again.

We form our opinions from life's experiences and from the knowledge we acquire along the way. Little knowledge equals little understanding. More knowledge equals more understanding. Much knowledge equals much understanding.

We've often heard it said that what we don't know can't hurt us. But in this case, I believe it can. I believe it does. I believe it hurts us all very badly.

FEEL THE HEAT

During an extreme heat wave I felt just how oppressive the heat can be. But there's one kind of oppression I have never felt personally, and that is the oppression that black people feel in this country every day.

The dictionary defines oppression as the unjust or cruel exercise of authority or power: a sense of heaviness or obstruction in the body or mind. It defines oppressive as unreasonably burdensome or severe: overpowering or depressing to the spirit or senses. To oppress means to suppress, to crush or burden by abuse of power or authority: to burden spiritually or mentally as if by pressure: to weigh down.

Most of us have heard "Why don't black people just pull themselves up by their boot straps?" or "Why don't they just work hard like everybody else?"

Perhaps if I experienced oppression for a day, a week, a month, or a year, I might begin to understand what it's like to have someone trying to "keep you down.' How well would I function on my job if I constantly felt a sense of heaviness in my body and mind? I don't know. I've always had a sense of lightness and happiness. How well would I perform my daily duties if I were burdened spiritually or mentally? I don't know. I've been at peace with my creator for as long as I can remember and my mind has always been free.

Unless and until we have tasted oppression, how can we be so condemning? How can we be so spiteful, hateful, and critical? How can we deny reparations if there is a chance it would make life better?

I know, many of us say our ancestors were not slave owners and neither are we. We are not the guilty ones. We do not owe reparations. But if we are not guilty of sins of commission, are we guilty of sins of omission? I'll always remember a quote I read when I was nineteen years old. "The only thing necessary for evil to triumph is that good men do nothing." I personally replace the word evil with the word racism and find it just as true.

Haven't we all done NOTHING long enough?

RID YOUR COUNTRY OF PREJUDICE

To anyone who feels compelled to begin making changes where they live, I offer the following:

We must learn to guard our thoughts. We must erase the negative and propel the positive. Vibrations are powerful forces that are too often used for evil. We must consciously and purposely expel the falsehoods and negative thinking from our minds. We must consciously and purposely replace them with truth and positive thinking.

We must learn (or re-learn if we have been incorrectly taught) black history. White people must know about the terrible atrocities that took place during slavery. They must know about the incredible accomplishments of black people in spite of years of oppression. They must know about the glorious history of Africans before slavery. They must know about the remarkable people who have paved the way for the reclaiming of their greatness.

We must have the courage to walk away from ethnic jokes and to openly rebuke those who create tension through their words, actions or stares. We must no longer be silent. We must stop being willing or unwilling participants in racially motivated acts of oppression. We must invite black people into our homes. We must get to know them. We must shake each other's hands and weep bitter tears together for the years of separation our misunderstanding has caused. I believe it is time for us to look each other in the eyes. So many of us turn away from each other, cross the streets to avoid each other, busy ourselves nervously when approached. I believe it is time for us to sit down across a table from each other and stay there until we have touched that spark of humanity we all share, then to rise up and together light the torch which will blind the eyes of prejudice and hatred in our country forever.

FERGUSON

I had fallen out of the letter writing habit for a while but events in Ferguson inspired me to let my voice be heard once again.

As a child, I live in Palmyra, MO for a number of years. We had exactly two Black kids in our school and I was given very strict instructions to stay away from them.

"Black people need the gospel too, dear," I was told. "We just can't associate with them. I never have figured that one out, but after years of marriage to a black man, I have definitely figured out a few important things about race relations in America.

The first thing is that most white people do not know how to listen to black people. I don't mean just hearing the spoken words, but hearing and understanding the unspoken meaning behind them.

We white folks need to listen to the pain, the frustration and the emotions now boiling over like a lid being blown off a pressure cooker.

The killing of unarmed black men by police officers takes place over and over and over again. Tears are shed. Speeches are said. Then life goes on for most people as if nothing even happened. Laws don't change, policing doesn't change, and accountability doesn't change. The only thing that changes is life for the loved ones the victims left behind.

Secondly, I believe we need to openly recognize and admit that white racism is essentially responsible for many of our problems. The main problem being the racial attitude and behavior of white Americans towards Black Americans.

Third, once we have listened and finally admitted our racism and its' far reaching consequences, we must stop placing blame, embrace the truth- no matter how painful-and press forward together towards not only tolerance, but forgiveness, unity and love.

HAPPY BIRTHDAY

I am writing this on my birthday, Dec. 4th, 2014. But while doing so, I am thinking of Michael Brown, Eric Garner, Tamir Rice and John Crawford III.

I am white. They are all black. They are all dead. And none of them died of old age like I fully expect to do. They died because of what was in the minds of their killers. A perception that they were violent, unredeemable animals. That their lives do not matter. That their lives have no value. I can think of no other reasonable explanation for their deaths.

When I was in my early twenties, I was attacked, thrown down a flight of stairs and threatened with rape. My attacker was a young black man we called Frosty. I was, miraculously, unharmed. When I went to the police station, the cops kept saying, "Don't worry. We'll get this critter." Critter?

For the next few days I had trouble sleeping. Every night when I closed my eyes I would see Frosty's angry, black face coming towards me. But in the light of the next morning, I would also see the faces of Brother Sam, Brother Joe, Brother Charles and Brother Matt. They were all wonderful black men I'd come to know and love at my church.

Frosty was one black man. One black man that scared me. One black man that threatened me. But could I say from then on that black men were violent? No, just that Frosty was. Could I say from then on that black men are scary? No, just that Frosty was.

As an individual I have learned from this and many other experiences that I cannot and must not stereotype black men. I know there are some scary, very bad black men. But I also know there are some very good black men. In 1980 I married one. Please, please, let's get above and beyond our long held prejudices. I truly believe that all of our lives depend on it.

CELEBRITY

I read an article where the white writer believed that if Black folks were to become educated and wealthier, then folks would find it easier to get along with them. Thus, race relations would greatly improve.

Then I read a Jet magazine article about black celebrities who had done just that – gotten educated, wealthy and even famous. And their encounters with racial prejudice sent the message that no matter how much they accomplish or how well they are received in society, there are still many white people who view them in stereotypes.

Actor and performer Debbie Allen recalled being snubbed by a white salesperson in a jewelry store. Vanessa Williams was mistaken for a server at a reception after she had just sung for the president at Ford Theatre. Olympic gold medalist Al Joyner was pulled over and handcuffed twice by L.A. police looking for hit and run driver. "To know this happened because of the color of my skin," he said, 'that hurts."

These black celebrities have realized that despite the advantages of the Civil Rights Movement, prestigious jobs, luxury cars, and the trappings of success, there are still whites who feel that blacks are servants or criminals.

What I believe will have the greatest effect on race relations is for white people to understand that they are the ones with the problem. We are the ones who need the changing. We are the ones who need the dialogue. Economic success, while certainly beneficial, will not change hearts, minds or perceptions. Only honest, difficult, face to face conversation will.

LISTEN

One year there were many race related problems in the Grays Ferry section of Philadelphia. The issues prompted me to look up the word racism in the New World Dictionary. I found this meaning, "a belief that race is the primary determinate of human traits and capacities and that racial differences produce an inherent superiority of a particular race."

I realize that pointing out the existence of racism and the need to discuss it stirs up sensitivities on both sides. I also realize the need to admit that the white race in this country has historically seen itself as superior to other races, particularly the black race.

I have been privileged in my life to be shown "the other side." I am white and have been married to a black man for 36 years. We have two bi-racial children. While I have experienced the ugliness of being hated and mistreated for who I am, I do not consider that experiencing racism. When a black person is hostile towards me, I do not view it as racism against me. I do not like it. I do not run from it. I deal with it as best I can. But I do not consider it racism.

I do consider this. African Americans who are descendants of slaves, cross paths with descendants of slave owners every day. Descendants of the people who bought and sold their ancestors. Descendants of the people who raped, whipped and murdered their ancestors. Descendants of the very ones who owned their ancestors, and treated them like animals, considering them 3/5 human. And now they are their teachers, their employers, their merchants, the neighbors and their co-workers.

And unfortunately, even now, many still carry ingrained attitudes of superiority with them, consciously or unconsciously. And just as unfortunately, these attitudes are conveyed in many subtle, unspoken terms. (Some whites turned their backs on peaceful black demonstrators in Grays Ferry. What message did that send?)

When I married my husband, the first thing he said to me was "Listen." And I did. I listened to his experiences, his point of view, his insights. Years later I'm still listening and learning.

I now believe that the biggest difficulty in race relations lies in the inability of white people to listen to black people. I mean really listen. Without criticizing. Without defending. Without interfering. Without interjecting our values, our opinions, and our view point. You see, most of us still see life from the view of the oppressor. And from that standpoint, we will never fully understand the views and actions of the oppressed.

Truly Free
(a poem by Delores Paulk)

Within the tunnels of my soul

there lives a hope that one sweet day

before the ignorance of hatred

eats away the innocence

I cherished as a child,

The light of truth will shatter

All the darkness that has made me creep

Along the walls of prejudice

And set me truly free.

Emancipation
(a poem by Delores Paulk)

A piece of paper, something written, words declared.

A proclamation, emancipation.

But what of laws unpenned by human hands

Yet etched within the hearts of those who held themselves

To be superior?

And what of fear for years instilled

In minds of humans so divine

They carried burdens for the world and sweetly sang?

Ah, day of victory be near

When pedestals of power, pride and prejudices fall

When brotherhoods of common cause appear

When moved by humbleness and love

We clasp our hands together you and I

And travel upward to the realm where

Fear is gone, where truth alone prevails

And written in our hearts the words

We are now truly free.

Somebody Has To Do Something

I was nine years old, and sitting in junior church. The lady up front said that we were not Christians because we came to church. That we were not Christians because our parents were. That we needed to make a personal decision to accept Jesus Christ as Lord and Savior of our own lives. And so I did. I raised my hand, went up to the front for prayer and officially became a believer. That day is still vivid in my memory.

I've since heard many stories of people who have searched and continue to search for faith in God. I've always felt that putting faith in my heavenly father was a simple thing for me because of the faith I had in my earthly father. He was always there, always dependable and always consistent. So it was an easy thing to transfer that faith to my unseen yet ever-present, spiritual father.

Because of my father's strictly conservative brand of Christianity, however, I discovered as I grew up that we differed on some things. He would often say "God said it. I believe it. That settles it." And for him I think things really were that fundamental. He would not read a book unless he knew that the author was a "good Christian" person, usually a man. When he closed his Bible, he closed his mind.

I was taught to believe whatever the minister preached. After all, he had studied the Word of God and he knew what it all meant. When I was fourteen I heard our pastor say that we should never do anything that looked like sin to anybody else. As an example he said that if he as a minister gave a ride home to a female church member and somebody saw them leave church together, that would not look good. So therefore he could not do it. I remember thinking how stupid that sounded to me. What's the lady supposed to do? Walk? But I kept it to myself because we were not to question the minster of God.

I remember a Sunday School teacher saying that God did not want us to intermarry with people of different races. I must have been a preteen at that time. I sort of agreed with her, saying something like "God would never lead me to do something that he himself was against."

Many years later when I was actually thinking I might marry a black man I asked my mother what she thought of the idea. She said, "I don't know. We were just always taught it was wrong."

When I was in elementary school, we lived in Palmyra, Missouri. There were two black guys in my school. I was told never to talk to them, so I didn't. I was also told that Black people needed the gospel too, but we were not allowed to associate with them. I never did figure that one out.

When I was in sixth grade we moved from Missouri, my father's place of birth, to Pennsylvania, my mother's home. We lived in Kinzer, and I went to Paradise Elementary School. I was a good kid, never got in trouble, and sang in the choir.

Later, at Pequea Valley High School I was known as one of the good girls. Everybody knew I went to church, and I was never ashamed of it. One girl even called me one of God's favorite sheep. I went to my church youth group meetings and formed a Bible quiz team with some kids at school. We went to monthly Youth for Christ meetings in Lancaster and passed out gospel tracts.

I remember basketball games, track meets, choir practices and performances, great friends and caring teachers. I remember discussions in classes when I spoke out about my faith in God. One English teacher told me she felt like she was blaspheming when she read my papers.

All through school I never doubted that God had something for me to do. I listened intently to sermons and read the Bible daily. Of course, living in the Pennsylvania Bible Belt, that was just doing what was expected of me.

But in the beautiful Bible Belt that was Lancaster County, racism just sort of hung in the air. Nobody talked about it. You just felt it. You just knew it was there. You did, of course, get the occasional comments like my dad used to make. "Black people want everything handed to them on a silver platter." Black people are lazy." Black men are dirty, oversexed and out to get white women."

I knew deep inside that there was more to being a Christian than going to church on Sunday. I remember sitting at the dining room table in my parent's house, looking at a newspaper. There was a picture of a black guy on the front page and a story about his arrest for some crime or other. I started to cry. "Somebody has to do something," I said. I just cried and cried and cried. It made no sense to me. I didn't even know this person. I had no idea what to do. I just knew that somebody had to do something.

HENRY

After graduating from high school, I got a job as a hostess in a hospital lunchroom and moved into a small apartment with a girlfriend. I also sang with a group called Maranatha Productions who did Christian concerts and plays.

When I was 18 years old I met a black man for the first time in my life. His name was Henry. He was a soloist with Maranatha, and he contradicted every stereotype I'd ever heard about black men. He was friendly, mannerly, clean, was not oversexed and sang like an angel.

The year I spent with that group was great. During that time I learned that many of the things I'd been taught about Black people were not true. It took a while for me to admit that my parents and even my church had given me false information.

I've figured out that at some point when we grow up, we must make a decision. We start thinking for ourselves or continue believing things just because we were taught them by people we loved.

Then I met another black guy named Ted. He came to the area from California and was heavily into what was called "The Jesus People" movement. He was tall and lanky and immediately took a liking to me.

We grew quite close and even imagined while we held hands, that one day we would show the world that blacks and whites could get along together. His group wasn't anything like Maranatha, and I gradually left one for the other.

Ted and I would go out and witness to young people, carry our Bibles everywhere, have meetings where everybody joined hands, sang songs and swayed. At one such event my father stormed in and demanded I leave these Pentecostals. Talk about embarrassed.

Anyway, Ted sometimes took me home at night, and then he'd come by early in the morning for breakfast. Of course, word got out that we were sleeping together (which wasn't technically true). Then my roommate moved out and I was couldn't afford to pay the rent. Oh, and Ted also moved on to another girlfriend.

Forced to move back in with my parents, I suffered a serious depression. I basically stayed in my room, didn't go out with friends or family at all. I remember my father telling me that I should pray, but I told him that I didn't feel like it. This was before depression was considered a treatable condition and I didn't go to a doctor or take medicine. I just sat there miserably for a month.

Then, one day I was reading a book, and it told me to praise God no matter how I felt. The author said that if I sang praises, even if I didn't feel like it, I would begin to feel better. So I did. I got up and started singing out loud. It was like a weight being lifted right off my shoulders. I started feeling better, and I started believing that things could actually get better.

The weird thing about this part of my life is that I actually had a blonde haired, blue eyed, boyfriend who had gone to Vietnam. When he first left, I wrote him lots of letters, but the longer he was gone, the farther I got from him emotionally.

He, of course, had no idea I'd forgotten about him. When he came over for the first time after his discharge, I had to tell him that I was sorry, but I couldn't be his girlfriend any more. It made him extremely sad and I felt awful, but I just kept saying "I don't want to be a run-of-the-mill, ordinary Christian. I have to do something. I have to do more. I don't want to just go to church on Sundays and then live like everybody else does. I have to do more."

I don't know how much of what I said made any sense to him, but we did break up and my life did begin to change.

TEEN HAVEN

I started going to Sunday night church services with a friend who lived in the city of Lancaster. One evening, they had a special speaker from a Christian Youth Organization called Teen Haven. They were opening a center right there in Lancaster and were looking for volunteers.

I went to the center the next week and helped them clean, wall-paper and paint. Later when the kids started coming, I taught them songs and took them places. After a month or so the founder of Teen Haven invited me to work in their Philadelphia center.

I told some friends I was moving to Philly and the first reaction I got was, "Hey, I've got a sawed off shotgun I'll sell you real cheap." A church friend said, "Philadelphia? Won't you be scared?" I don't remember anyone thinking it was a great idea.

I do remember the day my father took me to the train station. Mother stayed at home because it was too sad for her. Dad, however, was proud to have me going off to be essentially what he considered a missionary to the inner city. I had never even been on a train.

I don't remember a thing about the actual train ride. I suppose I read a book or fell asleep. I do, however, remember getting off the train in North Philadelphia and being greeted by Greg, a tall, young black guy with a huge afro. He tried to make me feel welcome and talked the whole way to the Teen Haven center.

He also tried to make me feel welcome by grabbing me and kissing me any time the director, Barb, wasn't around. He even told me that some of the guys in the "hood" wanted to "get with me." It's funny, but I remember thinking, "Oh, that's what the time with Ted was about. To get me ready for this." I could only imagine how I would have reacted to a black guy grabbing me and kissing me on the mouth if I hadn't already been kissed by Ted. Amazing how God prepares us for things we aren't even aware of yet.

My first days were filled with excitement and getting to know the neighborhood, planning Bible study groups, gearing up for weekend trips to camp and opening the recreation center each day. On one of my first walks around the block a little black kid threw a can at me and I remember thinking, "What did I ever do to him?" I had so much to learn.

The first lesson was going to be finding out what it was like to be a minority. My white face was one of about three on our whole block and it became obvious that some of the neighbors would rather they'd never seen it.

In my naivety, I couldn't understand why anyone would dislike me. I'd never done anything to anyone and I thought I was here to "help." Then I'd be hit with something like this. "Look, honey, if I was to go out to your Lancaster county and try to teach the Bible to little white kids, do you think they'd let their children come?"

And I heard this, "Yeah, I hear you talkin about your white god. But you haven't seen your mamma killed in front of you. It's hard, white lady. It's hard."

One black man said, "Give me a thousand dollars, then I'll believe in your white god."

A teenage girl told me, "We can't come to your Bible study if it's at night. There's too much gang warring out there. We don't go out after dark."

I remember a dark skinned man standing on the corner watching me pass out gospel tracts. He approached me and said, "See, you're always smiling. But I don't have nothin to smile about like you. It's easy for you to come in and talk to me about your God and then run back to your little house in the suburbs." I told him I was living at 20th & Poplar and he said, "Oh, then, you know my people."

Indeed I was just beginning to learn about "his" people. Even now, after 36 years of being married to a black man, I haven't stopped.

JOHNNIE

My parents were never wealthy, but we always had food on the table and mother was a great cook. She sewed clothes for us sometimes and because I was number six of eight kids, I wore a lot of hand-me-downs.

I guess you'd call my parents strict. When things got to where mother couldn't handle them, dad stepped in with his belt and whipped whoever needed it. My mother would say, "I'll tell you something one time. If you don't do what I say, I'll tell you again, with a warning. If you disobey again, you will get a spanking."

So we were always warned, and spankings were never given in anger nor were they extremely painful. But they did sincerely believe in the "spare the rod, spoil the child" scripture. As I grew up, I came to truly appreciate their loving discipline.

I remember evenings filled with family devotions after dinner, then homework and bed. We did have a TV, but only one, which we all shared and usually it was on the channel that our father wanted to watch.

I remember growing up loved, protected and cared for. So when I met a gang member named Johnnie I was not prepared for what he had to share.

He walked into our recreation center, sat down in front of a chess board and asked me if I played. I told him no, but I was sure someone else could. Then he said, "That's O.K., I just wanted to talk anyway."

From what I remember, the conversation went something like this:

" Wanna hear a story about my mom bein a junkie and my dad bein an alcoholic?"

"Sure Johnnie. I'm listening."

He picked up a chess piece and said, "My life was in checkmate a long time ago."

He looked so sad I tried to reassure him, "God loves you, Johnnie. And so do I."

"You don't care," he said as he got up. "Don't nobody love Johnnie and Johnnie don't love nobody. I could kill you right now and never even think about it."

I do remember feeling a bit shaken, but still I wanted to reach out to him.

"Do you want somebody to love you, Johnnie?" I asked.

"Hell, yes," he answered. And then he walked away.

And I never saw him again, because two nights later he was shot and killed in a bar just down the street. I heard that his mother said, "Oh well, you live by the sword, you die by the sword."

MEAN JEAN

After I'd been working at Teen Haven about a year I got what I call a rude awakening into the world of racism and discrimination. It came in the form of a letter from one of the kids I thought had become my friend. We called her Mean Jean.

Dee,

The other day I was on the bus and a little white boy spat at me and called me a nigger. Tears came to my eyes. Why must I be called a nigger? Don't I have a name? I remember the day I looked up that word in the dictionary and it said it meant ignorant. I know I'm not ignorant. But if you look up that word in the revised edition it means, Black Americans, Negroes. Why?

What I don't understand is when a black person calls me a nigger I'm all right. But when a white person calls me that name, it hurts bad. I was crying the pain and frustration. I felt the hate. The desire to hurt someone.

Sometimes I think of you. Wondering if you were not a Christian would you call me that name. Then I answer that dumb question. No, she lived in the country where there's very little. You now when you tell me you love me I always say, "no, you don't," I be serious. I mean it. Because I don't think a white person can love a black person. Take out the God love, would you love me still? Dee, the Lord is inside you. He loves me – not you. You care for me because He cares for me. You white Dee. I respect you. I can't say I love you because I don't know how to love. How can I mix love and hate together? The walls of anger are getting stronger. I'm tired of trying to love those people. I'm tired of trying to get their education. Dee, as I write this letter I'm in tears. Because I'm writing to you, which you are white and knowing you don't understand. Getting angry at myself. Hating myself because I'm turning away from God. It's like I'm second best to Him. Hey, wait a minute, those white people are first. Praying to Him, wanting Him to answer my prayers. Wondering does God love white people more than us. We been the white man's slaves. Most of our women been their whores. Did God look down on us? Dee, I love the Lord. But God is a spirit. A white spirit.

The only desire I have is to die. The Lord made me second best.
You know Dee, the first child I have I'm going to name him Nigger
so he won't have to learn the hurt I have. He'll think he's famous.
The wall that I have is getting stronger. It's going to take a stronger
miracle. But will your God even help? My mind is going through
some changes it wouldn't have to if white people would leave me
alone. I need prayer. Pray for my attitude. The hatred, the pain,
discomfort, the unlovable soul that I have. Maybe God will help
then. He'll listen to you – you're White!
Jean

FROSTY

Frosty was a young man who lived for a while at the Teen Haven center on North 20th Street. One day when I was alone at the Broad Street center, he came to the front door. "You shouldn't have sent me to jail, Miss Dee," he said.

I told him I didn't have anything to do with that, but he reached out and shoved me across the room and down the basement stairs.

"I'm gonna get over on you, but don't worry about feeling guilty about the sex part, cause I'm gonna kill you afterwards."

I begged him not to hurt me as he pushed me up against the wall. He pressed his big black body against mine and ran his hands along my thighs. I prayed out loud, turning my head from side to side as he kept trying to kiss me.

Then suddenly he changed. "You've always been real nice to me. I don't know why I treat you like a dog," he said. "O.K., give me some money and I might not hurt you."

I went to the desk, gave him some money and ran up the stairs and out the front door.

"If you're gonna call the cops, don't do it right away," he said as he pushed by me and walked away.

I leaned on the wall of the center and asked myself what in the world I was doing here. Maybe I should go back to Lancaster County where I was safe.

A few days later I told another staff member what happened and he insisted I go to the police. When I filed the report the officer said, "Don't worry, honey, we'll get this critter."

Even though I wanted Frosty punished I felt awful when I heard the word Critter.

Months later in court the judge asked Frosty, *"Young man, how do you plead?"*

"Guilty," he answered without hesitation.

His attorney looked at me and said, "I've never had a client do that before,"

The sentence was read, and court was dismissed. I felt absolutely terrible. Why had Frosty had such a rotten life? Why had he been abandoned by his parents, left to fend for himself and live in the filthy hallways of the project buildings?

All I could think was "Now, he's in jail, just where they always thought he should be."

ANGELS

I woke up one night to noise out on the street. "What's going on?" I shouted out to a man near the corner.

"People goin crazy around here, lady. That guy just fell out that second story window. I don't think it hurt him too much, though cause he was probly too drunk to feel anything."

"That's not the only thing," someone added. "That lady that lives across the street fell asleep with a cigarette in her mouth and set her couch on fire. She's gone too."

I went back to bed. The next morning after a restless night's sleep I discovered my radio and a few other electronic things were missing. I called the police. I knew there wasn't any chance of getting anything back, but needed to report that somebody had broken in.

"You are one lucky lady," an officer told me. "See these piles of matches on the floor? That's how they got around in the dark. There's one pile right outside your bedroom door."

Later some guy on the street hollered as I passed by, "Hey, I like your green pajamas!"

Scripture verses flooded my mind. "Surely He will save you from the fowler's snare and from the deadly pestilence. He will cover you with his feathers and under his wings you will find refuge. You will not fear the terror by night, nor the arrow that flies by day, nor the pestilence that stalks in the darkness: nor the plague that destroys the midday. A thousand shall fall at your side, ten thousand at your right hand, but it will not come near you. If you make the Most High your dwelling, even the Lord, who is my refuge, then no harm will befall you, no disaster will come near your tent. For He will give his angels charge over you to keep you in all your way."

The next day I saw a cop on the street and when I told him what I was doing in the city, he said, "God isn't in this place, Miss." "Oh, yes he is," I said with a smile.

HITCHHIKERS

I was driving home from teaching a Bible Study on a freezing cold night when I saw and picked up two black hitchhikers.
"Where are you headed?" I asked as they got in, one in front, one in back.
"22nd & Fairmount," one answered.
"What do you do?" I questioned.
"We work the streets," the guy in back said.
"Oh. I teach Bible studies," I said and continued driving in silence.
When I stopped on the right corner, the guy in the back jumped out, but the guy in front wanted to go on to the next block.
When I expected him to get out, he slid towards me and put his hand on my shoulder. "How'd you like to be my teacher?" he asked.
I jumped out of the car, but he was quick and grabbed me, putting a knife to my throat. I felt blood trickling down my neck.
Jesus, help me. Jesus, please help me.
"Get in the car, white bitch, or I'll cut your fuckin throat," he ordered.
I pictured what would happen if I got back in the car."I'll die," I whispered.
"What?" he asked.
"I'll die," I whispered again.
All of a sudden, out of nowhere there were headlights behind us. He dropped his hands and ran across the street yelling, "O.K., I'll see you tomorrow then."
Tears stung my eyes. I was trembling. *All I could think was, "Are you crazy? You're gonna get yourself killed if you stay in this place. Go back to the country where you belong."*
But, as I fell into the car and laid my head on the steering wheel, I heard the voice of God.
DELORES, DIDN'T I JUST PROVE THAT YOU ARE SAFE HERE? DON'T YOU KNOW THAT YOU ARE SAFE ANYWHERE BECAUSE I AM WITH YOU?
So I cried some more tears. Grateful, joyful ones. And when I looked up there were no headlights shining anywhere.

HATTIE

A teenage girl named Hattie was coming to Bible study regularly, and I thought we were friends, so when she approached me one day I was really caught off guard.

"I hate you, Dee," she said. "I was watching you just now and I really felt it. I hate you."

Wow, I thought we cared about each other.

"Give her some time," other kids said. "Her father has been feeding her stuff about slavery days and he's got her pretty angry. Just give her some time."

Several weeks passed and I didn't see her or hear from her. I was just about to give up. Then one night I walk into Bible Study and there she is. "It's O.K., now," she says. "I just read this book about slavery but I know it's not your fault. So it's O.K. now."

And it was. *Thank God.*

BE THAT FLOWER

I wrote this as a letter to people who supported me financially while I worked at Teen Haven.

She walks outside and steps into what has been called the "Asphalt Jungle," with its busy streets and sidewalks, tall buildings and unsightly piles of trash. Graffitti catches her eye as she walks by rows and rows of houses, some liveable, many abandoned. Is there any beauty? Any good?

Her mind wearies as police sirens remind her of the lawlessness surrounding her. Her ears tire of the noise as neighbors argue into the night and teenagers threaten one another. Their words cut deep into her heart. Can she really love them?

A voice within her says she's done enough. Besides, what thanks does she get? The kids sure don't appreciate all her noble sacrifices. What's the use?

She walks outside and sees a flower. Tiny, delicate and beautiful, growing up through a crack in the sidewalk. It looks so perfect, so untouched. It stretches upward toward the sun, soaking in its rays, releasing them in sweet perfume that penetrates the air. What pleasantness she feels as she beholds this lovely, silent testimony to the character of its creator. What hardness is pushed through before it reached that final stage of perfection.

A voice within her whispers, "Delores, be that flower. Bloom where I have planted you. Soak in my love and release it to the city around you."

LITTLE DEE

For a while there was a young black woman living at the Broad Street center with us. Hers was a very sad life. She'd had a pretty messed up childhood, having been abused by her grandfather. She had lots of anger and covered it up with lots of laughter. Since her name was also Delores and everybody called her Dee just like me, she became Little Dee to us.

I took her to a movie called "The Hiding Place" about Corrie Ten Boom, a prisoner in a German concentration camp. The theme was that the love of God could penetrate even hardened hearts. Forgiveness could melt frozen spirits.

On the way home, little Dee looked at me and said, "I've learned to love and not to hate."

Later that night the phone rang. Little Dee's 15 year old cousin had been shot and killed. She came to my room, threw herself on my bed, crying, "Tell me it's wrong to hate now, Dee. Tell me it's wrong to hate now. They killed him and I know who did it. Tell me it's wrong to hate now!"

"I'm sorry," I said, throwing my arms around her. "I'm so, so sorry." I could think of nothing else to say.

YOU WILL MARRY A BLACK MAN

I was kneeling by my bedroom window, looking down at the city streets, saying my prayers.

Lord, I want to be used to show your love to the city. I want people to know that blacks and whites can get along. That they really can love each other.

Then the answer came, YOU WILL BE USED.

Thank you, Lord. Please just show me what to do. How do I do it when so many of them won't listen?

YOU WILL MARRY A BLACK MAN.

What?

WHAT BETTER WAY TO SHOW THATLOVE CAN CONQUER HATE THAN TO BRING A WHITE WOMAN AND A BLACK MAN TOGETHER?

But I can't. I can't. What will my mother say? It will be too hard.

Silence.

Lord, Lord, where are you? You can't make me do this. Give me something else. You can't make me do this.

Silence.

I jumped up, crying and shaking. I rammed my fists into the wall. I was bleeding, hurting. I threw my fist into the air and shouted, "You can't make me do this!"

Night after night my bedroom became a battlefield. Night after night I was looking for another answer.

One week later I found the answer I was looking for. The peace that comes from total surrender.

You win. I'll do whatever you say, no matter how hard. You win.
And I went to sleep.

VICTORY

The interesting thing is that victory for God was actually victory for me. The next morning I felt better than I had in days. The sun was bright. I felt light hearted and just knew that everything was going to be O.K.

And to top it off, I was pretty sure I knew who the black guy was going to be. I'd been fond of this guy named Harry for a long time. He was one of the teenagers who came up in Teen Haven and then became a staff member. He was funny and kind and I was crazy about him. I never thought that anything would come of it, but now I saw things in a new light.

For his part, he did care about me in his own way, but the thought of having a white girlfriend scared him. We would get together in secret but we couldn't be open about our feelings for each other. It's funny, but now that I say that, I'm sure some of the kids knew what was going on.

One night Harry actually told me he wanted us to go together. I was thrilled and saw this as a first step in what I was sure would end in marriage. But the first time we went out as a couple, I could see it wasn't going to work. He was just so uneasy and nervous. A week or so later he told me he was sorry, but he just couldn't do it. He told his cousin that everything would be perfect if only I was black.

Well, he started dating black girls and every time I saw him my heart would break. He still wanted to be friends, but my emotions were totally torn apart. I was really having a hard time figuring out what God was trying to do.

One night I was so upset that I called my sister, Evie, who lived out in Lancaster County. I asked her if she could come and pick me up, that I needed some time away. Her husband, Gary, dropped everything and drove the whole way to the city to get me.

I spent two days at their house, reading my Bible and praying. The amazing thing was that neither one of them asked me what was going on. They just left me alone. I was always grateful to them for that. I'm not even sure how I would have explained what I was going through.

Eventually, I got myself together and went back to work. I kept busy and decided that I just had to trust God with this part of my life. But I knew in my heart, that when Mr. Right finally did come along, he would not be white.

TIME TO GO

I'd spent 7 years at Teen Haven, during which time I drove a 74 passenger school bus to our camp in the country, taught Bible studies, trained Junior Counselors and directed the girl's camp program.

Some weekends I would drive my own car out to my parent's house with a load of kids. I have to admit that over time my father began to change and actually enjoyed having these inner city black kids running around in his front yard.

I'd seen many miracles during my time as a Teen Haven staff member, and my faith had been strengthened. My years there had been wonderful, frightening, empowering and exhausting. All kinds of things. But I began to get the feeling that they were about to end. I was driving my car to Lancaster. It was a beautiful day. I was alone. I was looking up at the huge clouds in the sky. And I heard God speak to me. "If I ask you to leave Teen Haven, will you go?" My eyes filled with tears. I could barely see the road. I was overwhelmed with emotion. I loved Teen Haven and the kids so much. I saw their faces in my mind. How could I leave them? They're still so young. They still need so much love and guidance. But I'd gotten the message, and this time I was not prepared to do battle with the Lord. I just wiped my tears, looked up to heaven and said, "Yes."

It wasn't easy to say goodbye, but I actually started looking forward to being just Delores Buckwalter, not Miss Dee from Teen Haven. I was going to be on my own in the city, not part of a Christian organization. I was going to live alone, not in a teen center. I was going to have to put my faith into action.

MEET PETE

I found an apartment in Germantown and got a job as a secretary at the Grand Old Gospel Fellowship radio show, hosted by a black minister.

I was an active member of the Germantown Christian Assembly and sang with their choir. I made a good friend there named Joyce and she called me her personal guru. She often came to me with questions about God and faith and the Christian life. I found myself helping a lot of people because I was so secure in my faith and so confident in my relationship with God. People found that a comforting trait in a friend.

I've always thanked God that I became a Christian so young and found faith at such an early age. I've always been grateful to my parents for showing me the way to a meaningful relationship with God. Now I was about to be taken to a whole new level of trust.

After work I often walked around the neighborhood for some exercise. One day I found myself surrounded by a group of young black men. I smiled and said hi and kept walking. I didn't know what was going to happen, so as usual, I prayed a silent prayer. Finally one of them touched my arm. When I didn't flinch or back away, he looked at the others and said, "She's O.K. man, leave her alone." And they all walked away.

One day while I was walking home from the grocery store, I heard somebody call out to me. "Hey," he said, "What's your name?"

I turned my head and saw a black man sitting on the steps. I'd seen him there before but never paid much attention. Now I looked at him closely. He was wearing jeans that needed washing. He was holding a cigarette in one hand and a bottle in the other. His hair and beard were a matted mess.

"Delores," I answered him.

"I'm Pete," he said. "Why don't you come over and talk to me some time?" And then he smiled. There was a huge gap between his two front teeth. Something warm washed over me. It was the friendliest smile I'd ever seen in my life.

"O.K.," I told him, "I will."

As I crossed the street, the heavens seemed to open up. HE'S THE ONE, YOU KNOW. HE'S THE ONE YOU'LL MARRY.

I glanced back at Pete. "O.K." I said. I had learned not to argue.

TALK, TALK, TALK

The first chance I got I went over to the steps where Pete was sitting and talked to him. We didn't waste time on small talk because he was a very serious man. He told me about himself, what he'd been through as a black man and what he was going through every day. He also told me that he'd seen me once many years ago when I worked at the 69th Street Farmers Market. I knew it could be true because I used to drive a group of workers down from Lancaster County twice a week to work at a produce stand there. Pete said he used to make deliveries to the same place. "There was something about you," he said. "Every time I went there I hoped I would see you."

The second time I went over to see him I took him for a walk. It was quite a struggle for him since he'd been doing nothing but sitting on that step every day. He drank a lot of wine and smoked a lot of cigarettes, so he was not in the best of shape.

When I asked him what he was doing sitting on that step, he said that he was waiting. He said he had gotten so angry with everything that he was about to do something violent. "I was just so mad. I was about to become a hit man," he said.

"But I knew what I needed. I needed a good woman to cool me out. So I told "the man upstairs" that if there was a woman out there for me I shouldn't have to go nowhere. That I should be able to sit right here and she would come to me. I told him if she came to me, then I would believe...and here you come."

He told me that he was married and had kids but was getting divorced. My parents and everybody at church would have no doubt objected to my getting involved with a nearly divorced man. But the more time we spent together the more certain I was that he was indeed, the one. We did have our differences though. Other than the black-white thing, he was raised Catholic and I was protestant. He'd been raised in an orphanage and I was raised in a large family, with 7 siblings. I'd lived most of my life in the country and small towns, while he was born and raised right in the city. Oh yes, there was also an age difference. When we met, he was 43 and I was 28. All the makings of a good relationship, I'd say.

But I'd learned to deal directly with my creator and not to ask around for other folks' opinions about what I should do. So when Pete wanted to get married, I made my decision vertically and then simply told people what I'd done. Of course, not everyone in my family or church was convinced that running off to the justice of the peace was a good idea. And not everyone expected this mismatch to last. That was in 1980.

LESSONS

Pete and I talked all the time. Many of our conversation had to do with slavery and what black people go through today because of it. I was shocked when he explained things to me like the slave ships and the inner passage. He said there were islands where Africans were taken to be made into slaves. That the slave traders would rip open pregnant women's stomachs and kill them in front of their men. They beat, maimed, killed, anything at all to scare them into obedience.

Then he told me about what happened once they were actually sold into slavery on the plantations. Large black men were used as breeders to make more slave children for the slave master. Slave women were raped. Black men were whipped into submission. Many who dared to defy them were sold to other plantations, separated from families and loved ones.

He explained that there were "house niggers" and "field niggers." The ones who worked hard in the field weren't allowed in the house. The "house niggers" were cleaner and served the master and his family. The female "house niggers" were often the slave master's whores.

Believe it or not, this was all news to me. I told Pete that the only thing I heard about slavery was that blacks were brought here to pick cotton and since they sang while they worked, we got Negro Spirituals.

But Pete filled my mind with all kinds of knowledge and made me read all kinds of books I'd never heard of. We spent so many hours talking. Lots of time I fell asleep while he was still talking. But I loved hearing him talk. He had so much stuff inside of him. He'd been through so much in his life, and he finally had somebody who could "cool him out."

MC (mixed couple)

Once when Pete and I were walking down Broad Street together we heard somebody say "There goes an MC." When I asked Pete what that meant he said it meant mixed couple.

We used to go to a local school and play wall ball together. One day when we were finished, we sat down on the school steps to rest. We were probably wrapped in each other's arms.

A little kid walked up and stared at us. He said, "Are you two friends?"
"Yeah," Pete answered, "we're husband and wife."
"You mean you like each other?"
"We love each other," I said.
"But my dad says that white people don't like black people."
I walked over to him, squatted down beside him, and looked him in the eyes. "Honey," I said, "the truth is that some white people don't like black people."
"O.K.," he said. "Bye."

I have no idea whether seeing us together had any impact on that child's life. But, here we are 36 years later still showing the world that black and white can turn out right - together.

DAILY LIFE

Pete still drank liquor and smoked cigarettes. I often thought, here I was, a good Christian girl from Lancaster County hooked up with a stone street man. But we loved each other, and no matter what happened, I knew we belonged together.

Even when I was angry with him for coming home drunk, I knew deep inside that this was meant to be. I knew that whatever I was facing, it was for the ultimate good. I knew this man would teach me what I needed to know. I knew that I had the patience he needed from a mate to see him through as he fought his personal demons. He always told me "Dee, this isn't me. I just picked up all this stuff. I'm gonna quit all of it. These were just survival techniques I used to make it out there on the streets. After a while I won't need them and I'll get rid of them."

So after a drunken weekend, he'd be back to his normal self and explain to me that this was what I needed to see. This is what many black women went through with their men. Lots of black men drank to deal with oppression. To try to keep a hold of their own minds. To keep from going off and killing their white bosses, who kept putting them down, stealing their ideas, setting them up to look like thieves, paying them less than white guys and working them harder.

Pete would leave for work in the morning with that wide, friendly smile on his face. But sooner or later somebody would give him that "Uh, oh, here comes a black guy" look and he'd get angry all over again. He'd been made to look guilty of things he hadn't done on different jobs. He was tired of having to work for white men who didn't know as much as he did, but would never admit it.

And then he'd come home and complain. Boy, I got tired of listening to that. He'd cuss and he'd fuss and then he'd fall asleep. He was always so angry. So frustrated. "Why can't they just let me do my work?" he'd ask. "Why do they have to keep fuckin with my mind?" So my weekdays were filled with his complaints about crazy white guys and my weekends were filled with him getting drunk. There were times when I looked up to heaven and said, "Is this really what you had in mind? Are you sure about this?"

And there were times when I thought about getting out. But I knew in my heart it would never happen. There was something Pete and I had to do. There was something we had to share. So I hung in there. In April, 1988, our daughter Kristina was born, and our son James was born in December of 1989. I don't intend to make them a big part of this particular writing, but I have to share something each of them said.

Kristina came to me when she was just a little girl. She said, "Mommy, people call dad black, but his hair is black and his skin doesn't match it. And people call you white, but your blouse is white and your skin doesn't match that. Why don't they just call everybody brown or tan?"

James put these words in writing when he was just a little guy. "Mommy, thanks for saying yes to the things that are right and no to the things that are wrong."

Out of the mouth of babes.

RIGHT FROM WRONG

This is an excerpt from a 1992 issue of Parents Express magazine that I found amazing.

"If your child is old enough to recognize that skins come in many different colors, then she is old enough to begin learning that differences are O.K. A youngster's attitudes about race aren't formed in seventh grade civics class. They begin in toddlerhood. So let's head for the playroom. What do you see? Are there dolls of different colors? Little Duplo people with brown or pink faces? Storybooks with tales from India, or Vietnam, or Kenya, or Brazil? Is your video library limited to Disney Classics?

You see where we're going here. What about you? Are the Huxtables the only black family that has even been in your living room? Does color creep into your everyday conversation?

Family therapist Harry Aponte spoke of the "negative twist" that we see too often when children become aware of differences in race. "When it goes beyond noticing differences to seeing the outside person as not only different, but somehow less worthy and less human, then you're headed toward prejudice. Kids absorb that kind of attitude from parents, schoolmates and society in general."

Racial hatred isn't an issue for tomorrow. Talk to your kids today about race. About fairness. No matter how small, they are never too young. Even the sandbox set knows right from wrong. "

I echo the words of David Gergen in a May, 1992 U.S. News and World Report editorial. It appeared right after the controversial Rodney King verdict. "If we open our eyes to what we are becoming, and then act upon it, these terrible days will yet serve a higher purpose."

And in the words of Rodney King himself – "Can't we all just get along????????"

BIG MISTAKE

When my son was 17 years old he made the mistake of robbing a man of $40. He tried to run but the cops were called and showed up in just minutes. There must have been a dozen of them, all drawing their guns on him, shouting for him to get down.

Once he was on the pavement, they proceeded to kick him and beat him up. I got a call from the hospital late that night saying he was being taken to the ER.

Pete and I rushed over there and waited and waited. We were told he hadn't arrived yet, that the cops were on their way with him. While I sat in the ER an ambulance drove up and a gurney was pulled out. What I saw looked like a body covered in a white sheet. My first thought was "Oh, my God, I'm going to be one of those women whose son is killed by the cops." The lump in my throat was so big I could barely breathe. The Pete came over to me and said that the man brought in was not my son.

I still thought I was about to die. I still shook like a leaf. I still felt my heart pounding in my chest.

Later they did bring our son in and he had a concussion and a huge gash on his leg, plus lots of cuts and bruises. But he was alive.

I feel that at that time I was given the smallest, smallest insight into what black women feel when their sons are killed by the police. I feel that for the first time I began to move from having an intellectual knowledge that such things happen, to understanding the emotional impact of such events.

I believe that we as white people have been so far removed from these harsh realities, that it is time for us to start letting our hearts, not our minds, be our guide.

REPARATIONS

When the kids were little I took them to the reenactment of the Battle of Germantown a few blocks from our house. Every year we hear and read about this historic battle and are reminded of the many soldiers who lost their lives in the fight against the British. Around the same time I also read an article about "The Battle of New Market Heights."

Virginia Congressman Robert Scott wrote, "The Battle of New Market Heights forever refuted the fallacy that Blacks did not belong in the army. The bravery of these men was extraordinary."

The article said that for years the role of 14 Black soldiers in turning the tide of the Civil War had gone ignored. The event had been wiped from history books and most recognition of their bravery was removed from markers in the Virginia countryside.

In 1980 the House of Representatives authorized the U.S. Park service to spend $2.6 million to "properly recognize and interpret the role of Black soldiers in the Civil War." However, only one roadside marker identifies the battle site near Richmond and even the marker shows the lurking racial prejudice – the word Negro has a small "n."

I have to wonder how many other things have been removed from our history books. I have to wonder how many other atrocities have been covered up. I have to wonder why we don't owe someone some serious reparations, not just markers.

When I brought this idea up to a white friends years ago, his reaction was that he'd worked hard all his life and earned his own money. He damn sight didn't want to give any of it for reparations to black people.

I wrote him this: I was born to missionary parents in the hills of Kentucky. We always had a place to live and food to eat, but we had no luxuries. I started working part time when I was 13 and have worked ever since.

For every paycheck I get, however, money comes out of it before I even see it. Money that goes for politician's salaries, round-the-clock protection for past presidents, medical insurance for government employees. Money for public schools that goes to administrators instead of teachers and kids. Money for welfare, medicare and social security systems that are full of fraud. Money to lend to other countries even though our own debt is outrageous.

Our hard earned dollars have always been taxed and spent by folks who didn't earn it themselves, and it probably always will. I have no problem with sharing some with well deserving descendants of black slaves.

As writer Ta-neishi Coates said, it's great when we stop beating somebody with a stick, but what do we do to repair the injuries and damages we caused?

And while we hope for the government to do the right thing, we can all do what I call "Random Acts of Reparations." A small example is when I was at the grocery store and a young black man helped me put my bags in the car. I paid him, but then I saw him pick up a large case of bottled water and start walking. I opened my window and said, "Hey, how far are you going?" He said he just lived in the next block. I told him to hop in, I'd give him a ride.

I could tell by his surprised expression that it was a totally unexpected gesture. After all, most white women are afraid of young black men. They cross to the other side when they see them coming, and lock their car doors when they drive by them on the street. They don't invite them to get into their car.

Another time at the same store, a guy asked if he could help me load up but I told him I didn't have any change to pay him. He said, "Oh, well, I'll help you anyway." And he did. When he finished, I took the twenty dollar bill out of my wallet and gave it to him. "Wow, thanks a lot!" he said.

I am sure that each of these young men told somebody about that single experience they had with a white person. A positive experience. A good experience. A stereotype breaking experience.

There are many ways to do a Random Act of Reparation. Even if you don't live in a black neighborhood, you can find an on-line cause to support. You can find a black school that needs books, a black rec center that needs basketballs, a black nursery school that needs toys, a black church that needs the roof repaired. Or you can do it person to person like I do. "Random Acts of Kindness" was a big thing at one time. I believe "Random Acts of Reparations" should be the next big thing.

THEY ALL LOOK ALIKE

Over the years I've heard folks say that black people all look alike.
I've been thinking about why so many white people seem to think
this is true.

I've concluded that some people just never get close enough to black
people to see the differences. Some white people are so fearful of
blacks that they won't get anywhere near them. From a distance, any
group of people could look alike. It's only when we get up close that
we see the minor differences that make us individuals.

There are other differences that many white people never get close
enough to see. Black people do not all look alike, nor do they all
think alike, act alike or live alike. In this United States we have
black people who are from the south, from the north, from Africa,
from Jamaica and Haiti, from India, from South America, and so on.
Just because a person's skin is black, that does not mean he is an
African-American descendant of slaves.

By never getting close, white people miss the opportunity to get to
know some really wonderful people. There are black families living
in inner cities who are doing their best to raise their children with
values of respect, loyalty and devotion to God. They form
neighborhood organizations to fight crime, drug dealers and anyone
who would try to take over their communities.

They help each other, protect each other, pray for each other and
love each other. They have bonds of closeness and friendship that
strengthen with each battle against the evil that attempts to invade
their lives. I can't tell you how many times I've driven down the
street and seen a group of black folks holding hands in a circle and
praying out loud for our city.

These are black people who blow every negative stereotype out of
the water. These are black people who, given the chance would talk
to white people and explain the world they live in. Explain what it's
like to be black in America. These are black people who could
change things, not just for inner cities, but for the world.

They deal with people out of understanding, concern, love and spirituality. For they know first-hand what oppression can do. They know first-hand what hatred can do. They know first-hand what fear and distrust can go. I wish we all had the chance to see first-hand what a little love can do.

BUS RIDE

As I ride around the city on the bus, I'm often the only white person on it. Once I had an encounter with a young black man that sticks in my mind to this day.

He looked to be about twenty. His hair was uncombed, his face unshaven, his loose hanging clothes covered with dirt and grease. As he picked up a half smoked cigarette from the floor, he mumbled, throwing his head from side to side. His glassy eyes pierced through curious, condemning onlookers as they "passed by on the other side."

When he looked my way, I gave him a smile, and he responded with a grin. He sat down next to me and started talking. He mentioned that he had seen me at a bus stop one day and that I'd smiled at him then too. "Are you an angel?" he asked.

"No, just a person," I said.

"You know," he said, "all I ever wanted was a decent conversation. People sit and stare all the time. I remember my first bad experience like that. I was in second grade. I just want to talk to somebody with some common sense."

His stop came and I told him where to catch the next bus. Instead of getting right off, he stood in the door and mumbled. People trying to get on the bus started yelling, "Hey, come on. Hurry up. I have to get to work."

After he finally got off and my own stop came up the driver apologized to me. "I'm sorry about that ordeal, but I had my eye on him the whole time," he said.

"That's O.K.," I said, "it was really quite alright."

"I admired the way you handled him though," he added.

As I walked down the street my eyes filled with tears. It hit me all at once. The simple sincerity of the young man. The rudeness of the riders. The surprise of the driver upon seeing an act of kindness from one human being to another.

TV

Pete and I have always looked at a lot of TV shows about race related issues. One documentary we watched was about violence among inner city young people. I looked at these young black men with bandanas tied on their heads, cigarettes hanging out of their mouths and deadly assault weapons in their hands. I've forgotten pretty much of what was said, but one thing I will always remember. One boy looked into the camera and said, "Do people think we choose to live like this? This life is hell. It's kill or be killed. But nobody cares enough to do nothing for us, so that's the way it's gotta be."

Many adults fear today's young people, especially black young people. Many despise them, criticize them, and categorize them. They turn their backs on them, throw their hands. If they wanna live like that let em live like that, we say.

I believe we need to take a closer look. We need to look beyond the outside and look into the heart. And when we do, we'll find that although they're tough on the outside – on the inside, they're just like us. Whatever our race. Wherever we live. Just looking for a little bit of genuine love.

But how many of us reach out? How many of us enter their world and dare to make a difference? How many of us care that much? How many of us love that much?

A friend of mine said that it's hard to make a positive impact on the lives of kids who are surrounded by negativity. I agreed. And I'll be the first to admit that sometimes I feel like closing my eyes to all of God's children, but my own. But as I walked away I said to him, "I look at it this way. You either try – or you don't"

And may God help us all if we don't.

QUOTES FROM YOUNG PEOPLE

In 1993 we watched an Oprah Winfrey show called "Shadows of a Single Protein." I wrote down a lot of what the young people she interviewed were saying. That was years ago and it startles me how true the statements are today.

1. Racism is still alive. It's just put in the background.
2. We are still looked at as 3/5 of a person. They started that in 1865 and politically speaking, they still believe it.
3. The people running this country are predominantly white and they're really messing up. They should really look and open their eyes.
4. If your white skin is so beautiful why do you lay on the beach trying to get brown? Why do you get collagen injected in your lips to make them bigger and tell me mine are too big? If being white is so great, why don't you stay white?
5. You're treated as an animal. Times have changed, but not for the better.
6. They're playing us all like a chessboard. Racism is on the dollar bill. It's there.
7. The people in power are the ones who can be racist. If you're not in power, what can you do?
8. I want to know what it's like to live in a world of people like me.
9. The deeds of the white people on our people - that's hate.
10. I hope America is waking up so riots won't happen again.
11. What bothers me is when I get on the train people move away from me. I wanna say, "look, I'm not gonna hurt you or rob you." But what good would it do?
12. People stereotype and look at you funny. They see us as people who sell crack, have drive by shootings. Sure, we got some of that, but they need to investigate and see the struggles young black men are going through. Why is he

selling crack? What problems drove him to it? People have given up on life.

13. Inside me I'm a real angry person. Two words people call me "boy" and "nigger." When I hear them something inside me snaps.

14. What keeps racism alive is that it goes on from one generation to the next.

15. Free your mind and the rest will follow. Don't be so shallow.

16. Why are we seeing color? We're all a person.

17. We all have work to do within ourselves.

18. Lack of self-respect causes racism. What you do to others comes back to you. When they call me names I laugh because they so immature to do that.

19. Everyone should know who you are. You're can't know who you are if everyone is the same.

20. Learn about differences. Break down fear.

21. Anybody that's racist should just get out.

22. We need to think about each other in terms of who we are inside. In order to understand me you have to know me. Black people aren't taught who we are. Without a black history there is no white history. Why is it we have to know their history but their history but they don't have to know ours?

23. The government thought it was easier to get rid of us. The text books make it seem like it wasn't so bad. Come up and talk to me. See what kind of person I am. I might be different but I'm not bad. Not lower than you. Not better then you.

24. Television is the drug of the nation. It has an unconscious affect. You know, I don't look like that person and because I don't I'm less beautiful. The idealized person is white and blonde.

REALLY?

When I first got onto social media in 2016 I was surprised by the wealth of information available and the things being discussed.
I read a National Review article about why race relations are getting worse. I found the article interesting, and it did give me some insights into some historical happenings. However, even more intriguing to me were the pages of comments following the article. One guy stated, "White failure to empathize with black problems is responsible for all the problems in the black community? Good grief. Black behavior is responsible for problems in the Black community."
Pete and I had recently watched a T.V. show called "United Shades of America." The host is a black guy and he visited a KKK leader and was given a tour of their compound. As the leader talked about all the problems created by black people, the host said, "But white people brought them here. They created the initial situation." The KKK leader said calmly, "But they were never intended to be our equal."
The intent of our founding fathers was to keep black people enslaved **forever**. The government not only sanctioned, but created institutional racism as a way of keeping black people "in their place." And by the way, when there are similar problems in other communities, like white ones, do we blame them in the same way, with the same vengence?
I think that it is an easy thing for most of us to read stuff on line, think about it, then post a response. We never have to see the people we are addressing. We never see their body language or "pick up" negative vibes from them through the computer screen. There's no way to sense the true intent of written words that may have rumbling undertones when spoken out loud.
I would like to see much more face to face conversation. What if a black man said to a white man, "Do you have any idea what it's like to walk outside in the morning with a smile on your face and the first thing you see is a white lady clutching her purse and crossing to the other side? Do you have any idea how painful that is?"

Or suppose a white person says directly to a black person, "I am so tired of being called a racist just because I'm white. I've never done anything to black people. Slavery was years ago. Why don't you just get over it?"

We all have so much inside of us that never gets said in the right way to the right people. We rant and rave to our friends and like-minded people, we text and post away like mad just to get it off our chests. But where in the e-world does it go? Who gets helped? And who gets hurt?

RIGHT OR WRONG

The country got all bent out of shape when an NFL player refused to stand up during the national anthem. I read the words he said by way of explanation. "I refuse to stand up to show pride in a flag for a country that oppresses black people and people of color."
To me, that was a perfectly reasonable form of protest. Would they prefer him to start riots, shoot law enforcement officers, post ugly pictures on the internet? Would they prefer him to rant and rave, curse and swear? Throw his fists up in the air and threaten to physically retaliate for the years of oppression his people have suffered?
Why, when our oppression of black people is brought up, do we attack the spokesperson? Why do we not look deep into our past and repent? Why do we not look deep into our present policies, our present racialized criminal justice system, our racialized housing, education and healthcare systems? Why do we not feel badly that this young man even has to have hurt feelings like this?
To the blonde haired woman I watched yell and scream that Colin should just leave the country if he didn't like it, I say this. Are you Black? Have you even been discriminated against because you are Black? Ever been denied housing because you are Black? Ever been followed around the store when you shop because you are Black? Even been racially profiled because you are Black? Even been beaten, shot, terrorized because you are Black?
No, of course not. So, how can you even begin to understand what this young man has heard, seen and experienced as a black man in these United States of America? And how can you even begin to understand the courage it took for him to do this one simple thing in front of the entire world?

WHITE SUPREMACY

I read an article that someone posted about some white supremacy groups and their hateful words and attitudes. Today I just keep wondering which parts of our history attest to our innate superiority. Was it when we came to new shores, found people already here and massacred them so we could take their land? Was it when we brought slaves over from other countries to build this country after we stole it? Was it when we whipped them, maimed them, raped them, brutalized them, murdered them?

Or was it when we fought a bloody civil war over the right to keep people enslaved? Or maybe afterward when we hunted and hung thousands of free individuals because we really didn't want them to be free? Or how about when we denied these same free people education, housing, jobs, land, or dignity?

Which of these actions, I ask everyone, are indications that we are of superior intellectual or moral character? Why, I ask everyone, if we were so superior, did we need to capture and kill people to start this country? Why did we not do it ourselves?????

I think of the wild, wild, west stories and how greedy land grabbers would take over whole towns and terrorize the good folks who just wanted a peaceful place to live and worship. I think of the money hungry men who brought in outsiders to build their railroads so they could get richer and richer and richer.

Now I know some will say that there have always been good white people opposing these actions and stepping up to help undo some of the wrongs. I agree. But, the fact that there are still so many white supremacy groups spewing out their hate, gives me pause. Why, I ask myself, and everyone else, has it taken us so long? Why are we not reaching the right people with the message of equality?

PAST

I read a book titled "Murder in Three Volumes," by Lorna Barrett. While it had nothing to do with racism, I found a couple sentences that made me stop and think.

One place a woman says of the local sheriff, "She blames me for something I never did. There's no way I can change her misperceptions of the past." Hmmm, misconceptions of the past. Our country has more than a few of those, I think.

Some of us seem to think that since slavery was abolished long ago, no one alive today is to blame, and racism disappeared with the Emancipation Proclamation.

Some of us seem to think that enough has been done to help the black population and that they should just "pull themselves up by their own bootstraps,"(never mind that they may not have any).

Some of us blame victims of institutional racism for the problems in inner city black neighborhoods (never mind the schools are underfunded, the jobs are shipped overseas, illegal drugs are funneled in, voting rights are threatened and decent housing is denied.)

Later in the book, there's this: "The guilt intensified. Perhaps if she hadn't asked Pammy to leave, Pammy might still be alive. Might: a word that held a lot of power."

Might we one day confess our guilt? Might we one day attempt to make things right? Might we one day come together, black and white, and stamp out racism once and for all?

I can all most hear the responses. And I do realize that there have always been white people working against racism. I consider myself such a person. I do, however, understand why many people still believe that "all whites are racist."

While some of us do not intellectually believe in our inherent superiority, if we were raised in America, we were raised in a racist society. And I personally believe that we have been influenced by that society to one degree or another.

Unless we had a most unusual and sheltered upbringing, we were exposed to certain stereotypes before we were even old enough to know what they were. Through not being encouraged to meet black people, by hearing derogatory statements, and seeing negative images in the media.

I believe we as white people are too quick to take offense and have our feelings hurt when others express their honest opinions. ("How can they say that? Don't they know what I've done?" "I marched with Dr. King." "I went to jail!") I've been there – felt that. But I got over it.

You see, I know me. And I do what I do because it is in me to do. I have written letters to the editor of local papers for years expressing my opinions about race relations based on my own experiences. Others can agree, disagree, approve, disapprove, congratulate or condemn. Well meaning whites must reach the point where we are neither pleased nor hurt by reactions to our efforts against racism. Then and only then, will we know that our motives are of the purest form.

Made in the USA
Columbia, SC
11 October 2017